the NOEL

CELEBRATING THE BIRTHDAY OF A KING

A READY TO SING CHRISTMAS!

Arranged by RUSSELL MAULDIN

Created by RUSSELL MAULDIN & SUE C. SMITH

Available Products:

Instrumentation

Flute 1, 2 • Oboe
Clarinet 1, 2
F Horn 1, 2 (Alto Sax)
Trumpet 1 • Trumpet 2, 3
Trombone 1, 2
(Tenor Sax/Baritone T.C.)
Trombone 3 • Tuba
Percussion • Harp
Violin 1, 2 • Viola
Cello • Bass
Synth String Reduction
Rhythm

BRENTWOOD MUSIC PUBLICATIONS

a division of

BRENTWOOD-BENSON
music publications

www.brentwoodbenson.com

MW01234278

CONTENTS

The Birthday of a King Medley

For unto Us a Child Is Born / Sing We Now of Christmas /
The Birthday of a King

Arranged by Russell Mauldin

4

SING WE NOW OF CHRISTMAS (Traditional French carol)

Sing we now of Christ-mas, No - el, sing we here!

Hear our grate - ful prais - es to the Babe so dear.

10

THE BIRTHDAY OF A KING (William H. Neidlinger)

Lyrics:
now No - el!_____

Al - le - lu - ia!_____ O how the an - gels sang. Al - le -

lu - ia! How it rang!___ And the sky was bright with a

11

Glory, Glory in the Highest

Words and Music by
RUSSELL MAULDIN and SUE C. SMITH
Arranged by Russell Mauldin

NARRATOR: *(Music starts)* What a wonderful story we have to share at Christmas. It begins with a people waiting for a Promised Son. It focuses on a young couple engaged to be married. It features a choir of angels, a band of shepherds, and a Baby sleeping in a manger filled with hay. *(Music changes)* There's a new star in the sky, kings from a distant land, and precious treasures. This is what we celebrate — the reason we sing, "Glory! Glory to God in highest!"

Sing the song of the birth of the Sav - ior.

Glo-ry, glo-ry in the

Come from heav - en to sleep in a man - ger.

high - est!

Tell the sto - ry of shep - herds who found Him.

Glo-ry, glo-ry in the

Tell the news of the star ___ that an-nounced Him.

high - est!

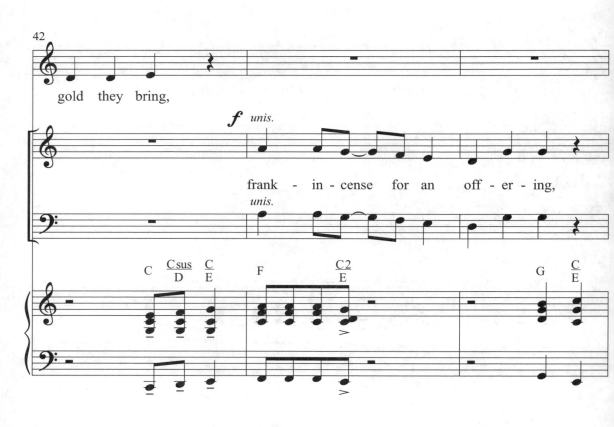

24

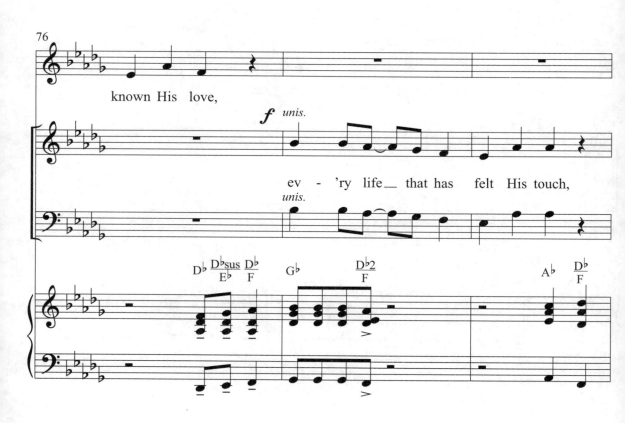

SPOKEN:
Sing the song of the birth of the Savior!

Come from heaven to sleep in a manger.

This is cause for a great celebration!

The First Noel

Traditional
Arranged by Russell Mauldin

NARRATOR: One of the most familiar carols of this season is a song of French origin that is centuries old. *(Music starts)* Its verses re-tell the entire Christmas story and they encourage us to give thanks to God for the incredible gift of His Son to be our Savior. The word "Noel" means Christmas, but it is also like singing "happy birthday." And what better way could there be to welcome our Lord than to join in singing a birthday song that celebrates His coming to earth!

sheep, on a cold win - ter's night___ that was___ so

deep. No - el,_____ No - el, No - el,_____ No -

el, born is the King___ of Is - ra -

Jesus, Born on This Day

Words and Music by
MARIAH CAREY
and WALTER AFANASIEFF
Arranged by Russell Mauldin

NARRATOR: *(Music starts)* Under any circumstances, the events surrounding the birth of Jesus would be dramatic. Mary and Joseph had already faced suspicion and scorn and danger. They had traveled far from home, and then Mary had to deliver her Son in a stable. Yet this story is so much more. The Baby was Immanuel — God With Us. He was the long-awaited Messiah. He was the Lamb of God, born to carry our sins to the cross.

Sing___ of His love to___ ev - 'ry - one. O

Je - sus,___ born on this day,_____

unis.

Je - sus,___ born on this day,___

unis.

heav - en - ly Child___ in a man - ger.___ O

heav - en - ly Child___ in a man - ger.___

Je - sus,___ born on this day,___

unis.

Je - sus,___ born on this day,___

unis.

48

50

Light of the Stable
with Angels We have Heard on High

Words and Music by
STEVE RHYMER
and ELIZABETH RHYMER
Arranged by Russell Mauldin

NARRATOR: *(Music starts)* The angel host filled the sky near Bethlehem with praise as they announced the Savior's arrival. Like those angels, we can't help but begin lifting our own joyful songs to honor Him. We proclaim that He is God, He is King, and He is welcome in our hearts.

58

prais - es.___ Hail! Hail!__ to the

guid - ing__ Light that brought us to - night to our

Sav - ior.__ Hal - le!_____ Hal-le - lu - jah!

In the First Light

Words and Music by
ROBERT KAUFLIN
Arranged by Russell Mauldin

NARRATOR: *(Music starts)* The helpless Baby who was laid in the manger that first Christmas night would grow up as the Son of a poor carpenter. *(Music changes)* He would reach manhood and begin a public ministry that would find Him going to the poor and the outcast, healing the sick, raising the dead, and demonstrating His power over the natural world. He would teach the people about God's love and show them by example what true greatness meant. His mission wouldn't be completed until it took Him to a cross, a grave, and a resurrection. And even then, His story would not be finished!

cried. But the heav - ens wrapped in won - der knew the

mean - ing of His birth. In the weak - ness of a

Ba - by, they knew God had come to earth.

ALL

Slightly faster (=84)

Am Em Am Em

Dm9 Em7 Am Em

Am Em Dm7 Em7 Am

mp

72

70

70

unis.

ba - by, but as the Lord of ev - 'ry man.

unis.

F#m7   Gmaj7   Em7   Dsus

73

rit. **ff**   *Broader* (♩=88)

Hear the an - gels as they're sing - ing on the

D   D/F#   *Broader* (♩=88) G   A   D/F#   G   A   D/F#
                                            B   C#

rit.   **ff**

76

unis.

morn - ing of His birth, but how much great - er will our

unis.

G   D/F#   D   A/C#   Asus/B   A   D/F#   G   A   D/F#

Jesus at the Center

Words and Music by
ADAM RANNEY, ISRAEL HOUGHTON
and MICAH MASSEY
Arranged by Russell Mauldin

NARRATOR: *(Music starts)* In our minds, the manger has become forever identified with Immanuel's coming. It's almost as if the spotlight of history shines on it so we can't ignore it or forget that at the very heart of Christmas, there is only this: Jesus, God's only begotten Son, was born for our salvation.

Je - sus at___ the cen - ter of___ it all. From be-

gin - ning to___ the end, it will al - ways be,___ it's al - ways been You,

Je - sus, Je - sus.

Je - sus, Je - sus. Noth-ing else

mat - ters. Noth-ing in this world will do.___

___ Je - sus, You're the cen - ter.

Optional Prayer / Invitation

NARRATOR or PASTOR:

Dear Savior, thank You for coming to earth so long ago. Thank You for the humble way You arrived and the news that was given that night, first to the shepherds, then to the wise men, then to all of us who would come after. The angel said, "A Savior has been born for you. He is the Messiah, the Lord!" Oh, what a gift You were, and what a precious gift it has always been to make You the center of everything we need, everything we know, everything that life is about.

Lord, there may be some here who have not found the joy and salvation that only You can bring. We pray that this will be the moment they whisper, "Jesus, be the center of my life today. Come into my heart and be Lord and Savior."

There may be others who have forgotten what it was like when they first knew Your tender love and mercy and they responded to it so readily. We pray that this will be the moment they'll reach out to You and say, "Jesus, be the center once more of everything I am."

Let us never come to Christmas without being intimately aware that You are the reason, the heart, the center of it all. We love You. We worship You. And we give ourselves to You anew, saying, "Jesus, You are the center of our joy."

We pray all this in Your beautiful name, amen.

Birthday of a King Finale

For unto Us a Child Is Born / The Birthday of a King / The First Noel

Arranged by Russell Mauldin

NARRATOR: Old Testament Scripture is rich with so many prophecies about the One that God would send to redeem us. *(Music starts)* And every one of them was fulfilled in the birth, life, death and resurrection of that little Baby born on that holy night. Our Savior has come and that is why we are filled with hope and joy!

90

Ev - er - last-ing Fa - ther, the Prince of Peace.____

Al - le -

lu - ia!____ O how the an - gels sang. Al - le - lu - ia! Al - le - lu - ia! How it

Broadly (♩=87)　　THE BIRTHDAY OF A KING (William H. Neidlinger)

87

94

THE FIRST NOEL (Traditional)